JUL – 3 2014

JASON MRAZ

D1232523

Cover Photo by Eric Morgensen

ISBN 978-1-4803-6707-4

HAL•LEONARD®
CORPORATION
7777 W. BLUEMOUND RD. P.O. BOX 13819 MILWAUKEE, WI 53213

In Australia Contact:
Hal Leonard Australia Pty. Ltd.
4 Lentara Court
Cheltenham, Victoria, 3192 Australia
Email: ausadmin@halleonard.com.au

For all works contained herein:
Unauthorized copying, arranging, adapting, recording, Internet posting, public performance,
or other distribution of the printed music in this publication is an infringement of copyright.
Infringers are liable under the law.

Visit Hal Leonard Online at
www.halleonard.com

STRUM AND PICK PATTERNS

This chart contains the suggested strum and pick patterns that are referred to by number at the beginning of each song in this book. The symbols ⊓ and ∨ in the strum patterns refer to down and up strokes, respectively. The letters in the pick patterns indicate which right-hand fingers play which strings.

p = thumb
i = index finger
m = middle finger
a = ring finger

For example; Pick Pattern 2
is played: thumb - index - middle - ring

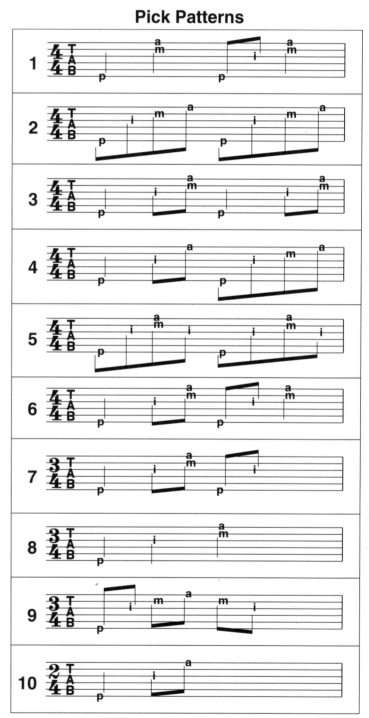

You can use the 3/4 Strum and Pick Patterns in songs written in compound meter (6/8, 9/8, 12/8, etc.). For example, you can accompany a song in 6/8 by playing the 3/4 pattern twice in each measure. The 4/4 Strum and Pick Patterns can be used for songs written in cut time (¢) by doubling the note time values in the patterns. Each pattern would therefore last two measures in cut time.

A Beautiful Mess

Words and Music by Jason Mraz, Mona Tavakoli, Chaska Potter, Mai Bloomfield and Becky Gebhardt

Copyright © 2008 Goo Eyed Music (ASCAP) and Raining Jane (ASCAP)
International Copyright Secured   All Rights Reserved

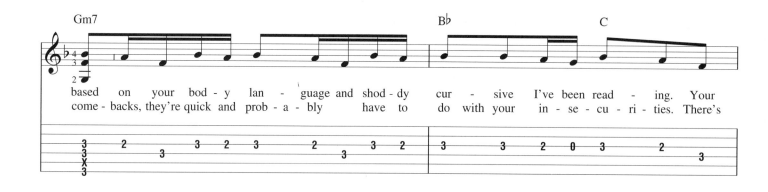

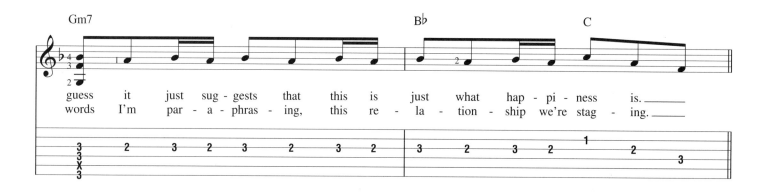

Pre-Chorus

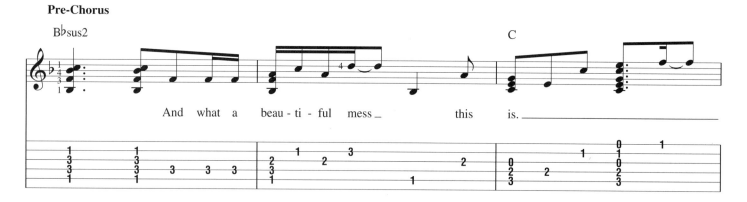

Butterfly

Words and Music by Jason Mraz

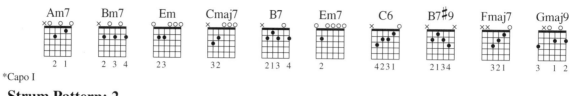

*Capo I

Strum Pattern: 2
Pick Pattern: 2

Intro
Moderately

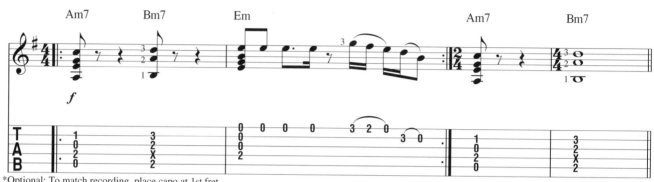

*Optional: To match recording, place capo at 1st fret.

Verse

1. I'm tak-ing a mo-ment, just i-mag-in-ing that I'm danc-ing with you.___ I'm your

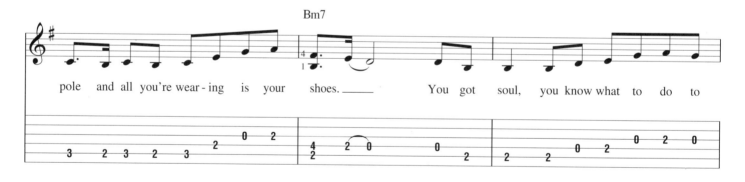

pole and all you're wear-ing is your shoes.___ You got soul, you know what to do to

turn me on ___ un-til I write a song a-bout___ you._____ And you have your

Copyright © 2008 Goo Eyed Music (ASCAP)
International Copyright Secured   All Rights Reserved

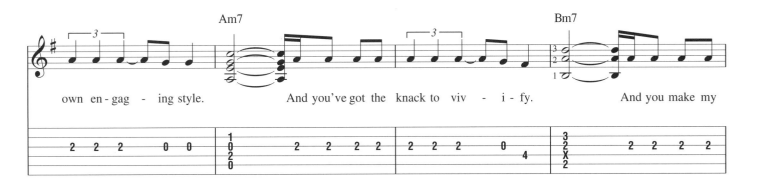

own en - gag - ing style. And you've got the knack to viv - i - fy. And you make my

slacks a lit - tle tight; you may un - fas - ten them if ___ you like. That's if you crash and spend the night. _ But you don't

% Chorus

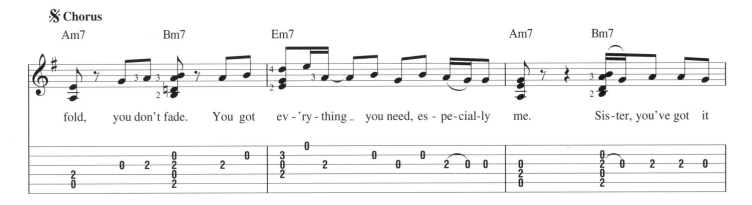

fold, you don't fade. You got ev - 'ry - thing _ you need, es - pe - cial - ly me. Sis - ter, you've got it

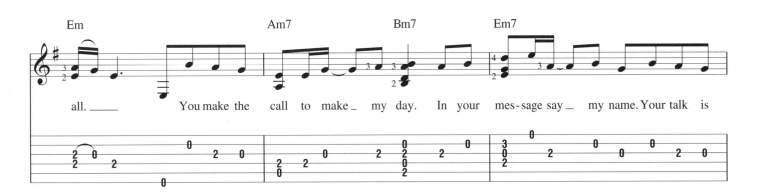

all. ____ You make the call to make _ my day. In your mes - sage say _ my name. Your talk is

To Coda 1 ⊕

all the talk. _ Sis - ter, you've got it all. ___

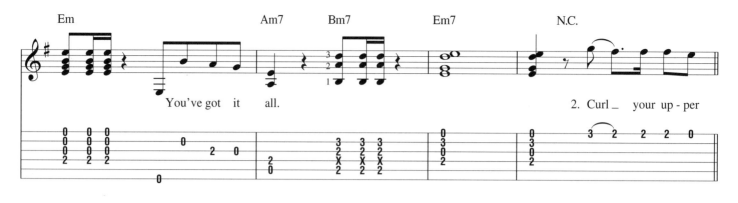

up - side down, slide in, slide out, slide o - ver here. Climb __ in - to my mouth now, child.

Interlude

Scat...

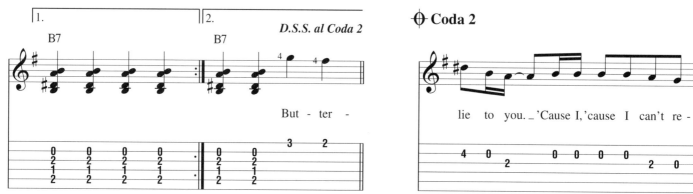

D.S.S. al Coda 2

But - ter -

⊕ Coda 2

lie to you. __ 'Cause I, 'cause I can't re -

Chorus

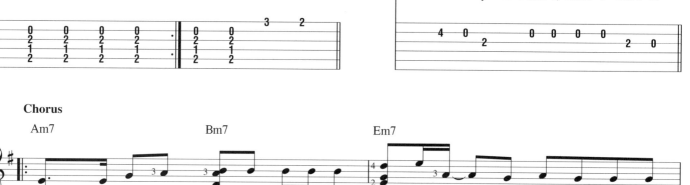

call a bet - ter day, sun com - ing to shine on the __ oc - ca - sion. You're an
for - tune fa - vors the brave. Well, let me get paid while I make you break - fast. The

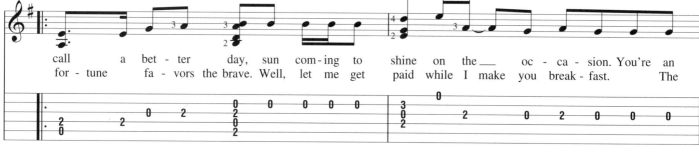

o - pen - mind - ed lady; you've got it all. _____ And I nev - er
rest is up to you. You make the call. _____ You make the

Additional Lyrics

Pre-Chorus 2 Well, you landed on my mind.
Damn right you landed on my ear and then you crawled inside.
And now I see you perfectly behind closed eyes.
I want to fly with you. And I don't want to lie to you.

I Won't Give Up

Words and Music by Jason Mraz and Michael Natter

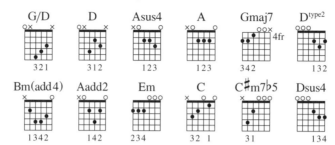

*Drop D tuning, capo II
(low to high) D-A-D-G-B-E

Strum Pattern: 7
Pick Pattern: 7

Intro
Moderately

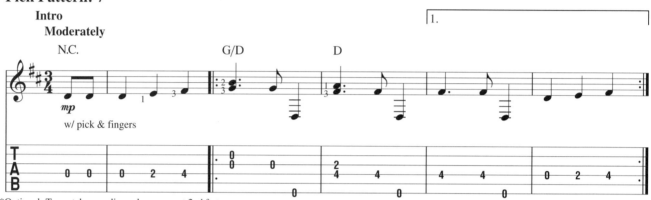

*Optional: To match recording, place capo at 2nd fret.

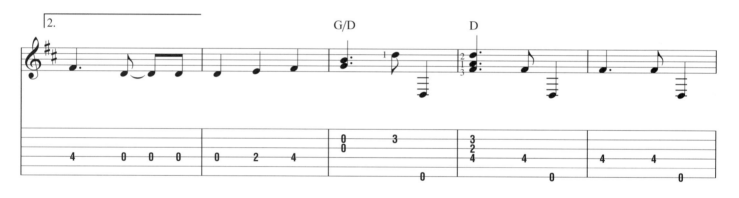

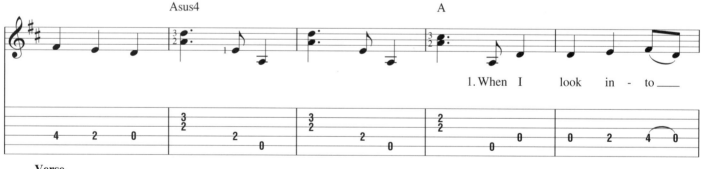

Verse

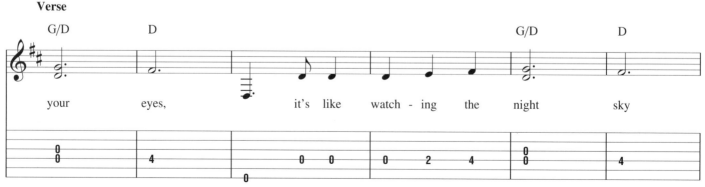

Copyright © 2012 Goo Eyed Music (ASCAP) and Great Hooks Music c/o No BS Publishing (ASCAP)
International Copyright Secured   All Rights Reserved

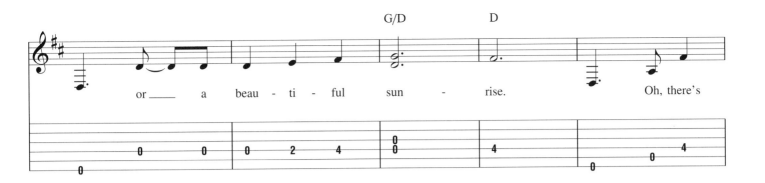

or ___ a beau - ti - ful sun - rise. Oh, there's

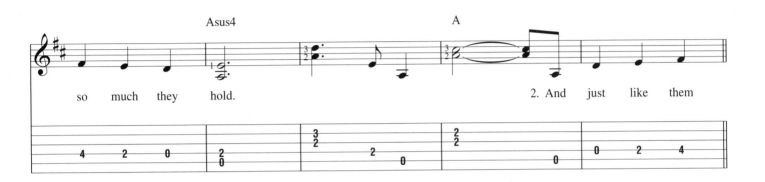

so much they hold. 2. And just like them

Verse

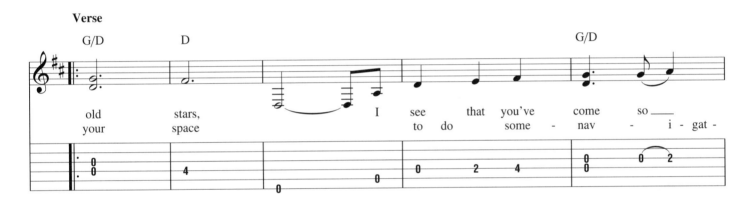

old stars,
your space

I see that you've come so ___
to do some - nav - i - gat -

far _____
- ing _____

to be right where _ you are.
I'll be here pa - tient - ly wait -

ing

How old is your soul? ___
to see what you find.

1. Well,
2. 'Cause

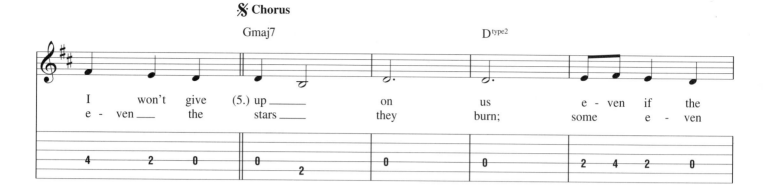

16

Bridge

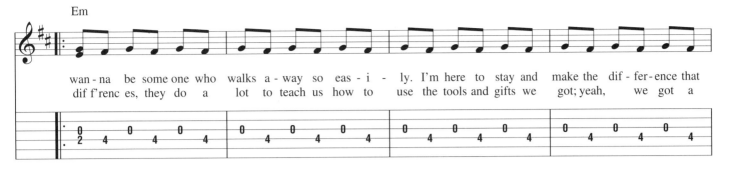

wan - na be some one who walks a - way so eas - i - ly. I'm here to stay and make the dif - fer - ence that

dif f'renc es, they do a lot to teach us how to use the tools and gifts we got; yeah, we got a

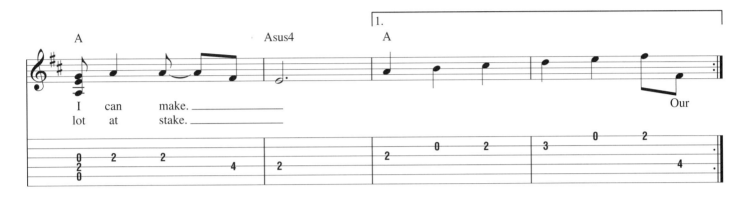

1.

I can make._____ Our

lot at stake._____

2.

And in the end, you're still my friend; at least we did in - tend for

us to work. We did - n't break; we did - n't burn. We had to learn how to bend

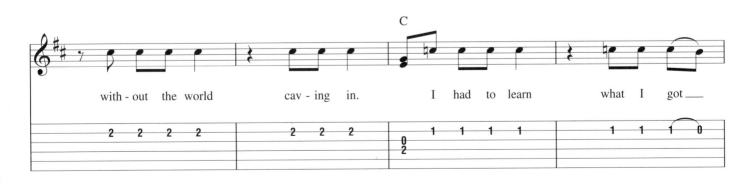

with - out the world cav - ing in. I had to learn what I got ____

and what I'm not _____ and who _ I am. _____

Chorus

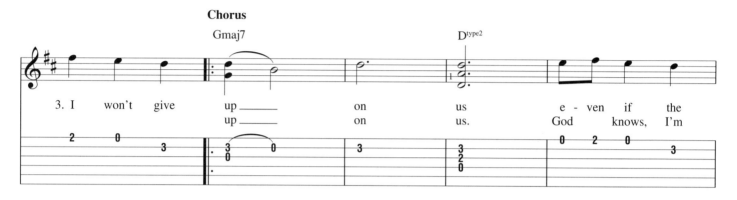

3. I won't give up _____ on us. even if the
up _____ on us. God knows, I'm

skies _____ get rough. _____ I'm giv-ing _____ you all _____
tough _____ e - nough. _ We've got _____ a lot _____

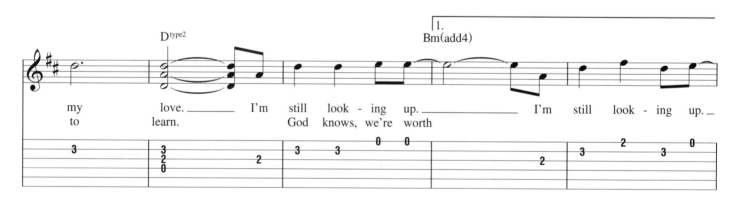

1.

my love. _____ I'm still look-ing up. _____ I'm still look-ing up. _
to learn. God knows, we're worth

D.S. al Fine

2.

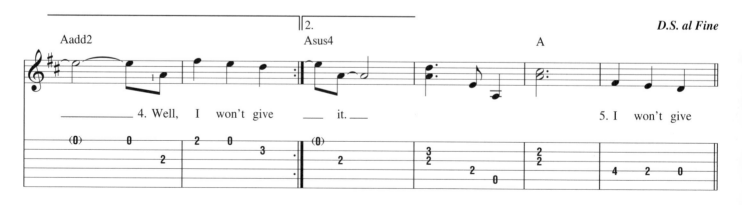

_____ 4. Well, I won't give ___ it. _ 5. I won't give

Live High

Words and Music by Jason Mraz

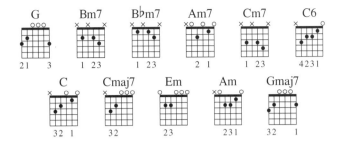

*Capo II

Strum Pattern: 5
Pick Pattern: 1

Intro
Moderately slow

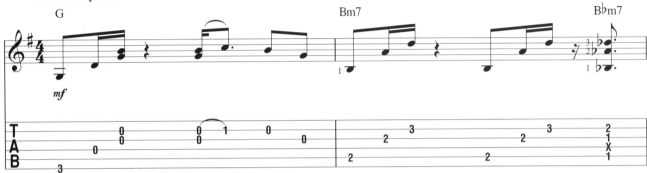

*Optional: To match recording, place capo at 2nd fret.

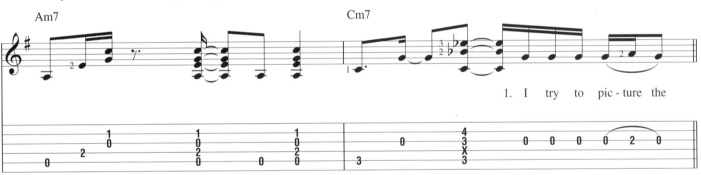

1. I try to pic-ture the

Verse

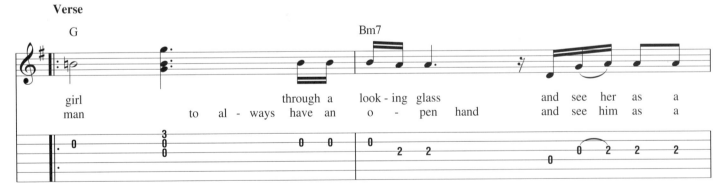

girl   through a   look-ing glass   and see her as   a
man   to al-ways have an   o-pen hand   and see him as   a

car-bon at-om.____   See her eyes____ and stare back at them. See that
giv-ing tree.   See him as mat - ter. Mat-ter of fact, he's not a

Copyright © 2008 Goo Eyed Music (ASCAP)
International Copyright Secured   All Rights Reserved

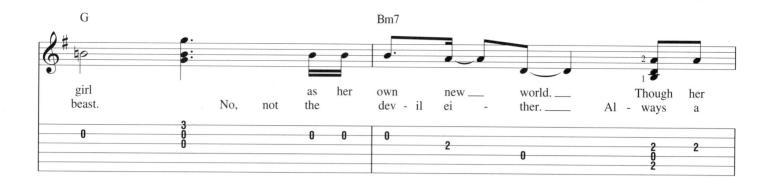

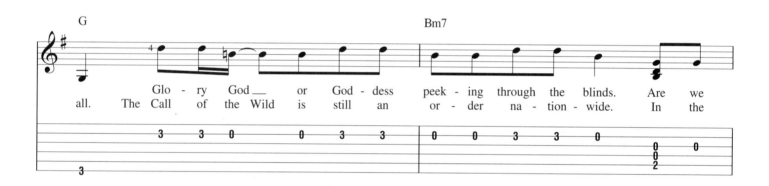

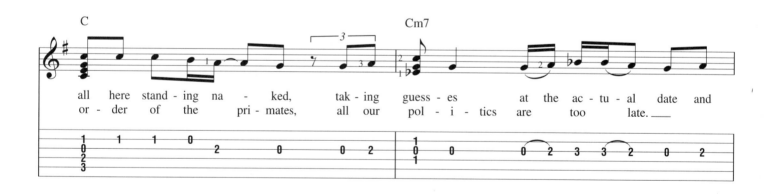

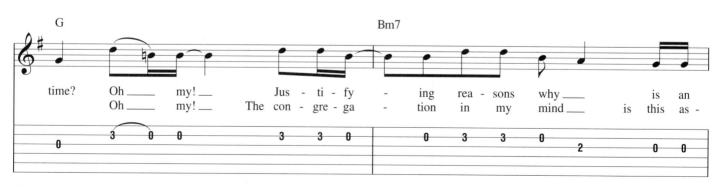

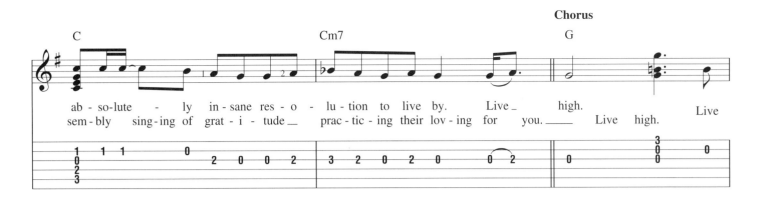

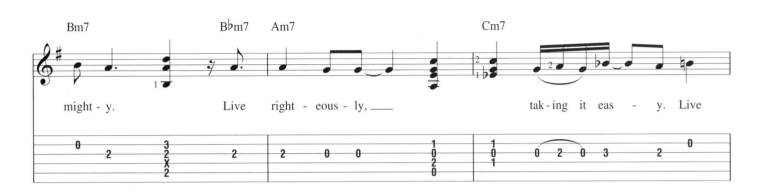

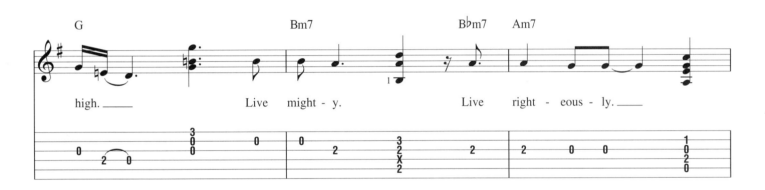

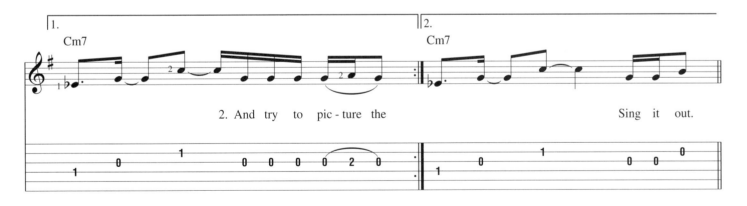

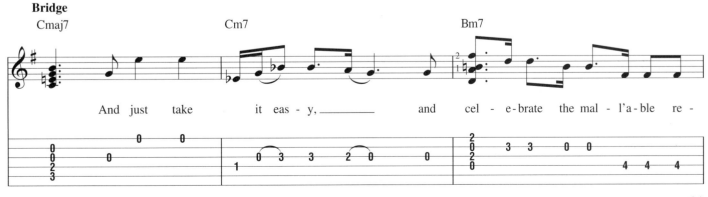

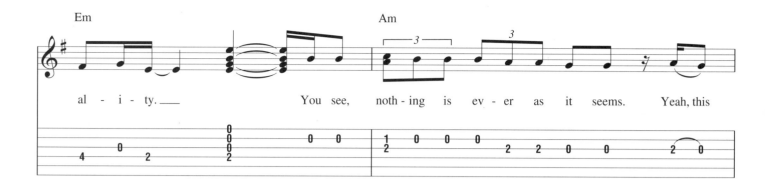

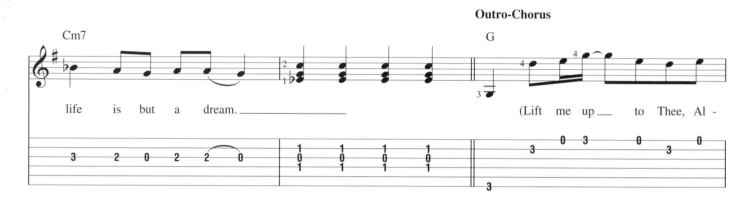

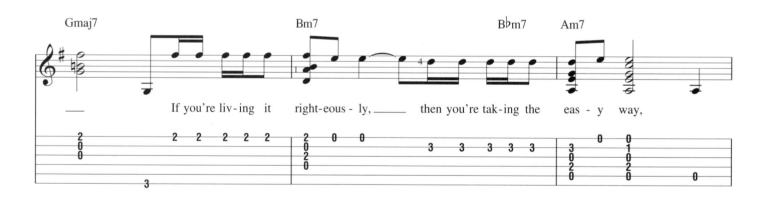

Freely

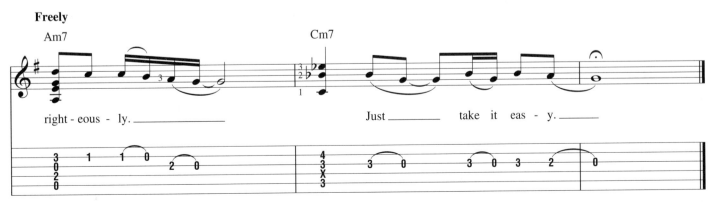

I'm Yours

Words and Music by Jason Mraz

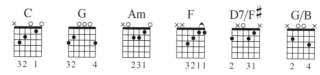

*Tune down 1/2 step:
(low to high) Eb-Ab-Db-Gb-Bb-Eb

Strum Pattern: 3
Pick Pattern: 1

Intro
Moderately slow, in 2

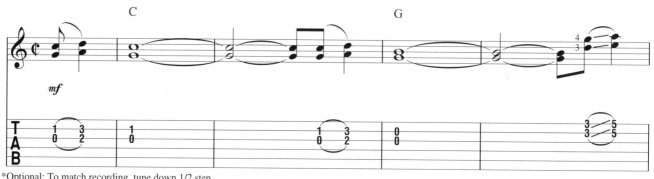

*Optional: To match recording, tune down 1/2 step.

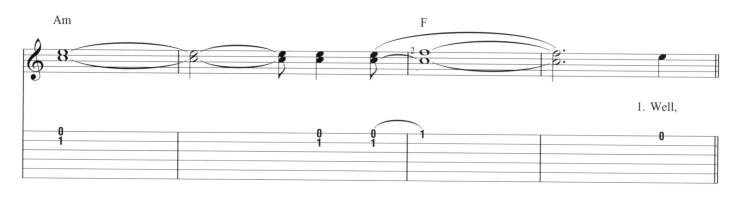

1. Well,

% Verse

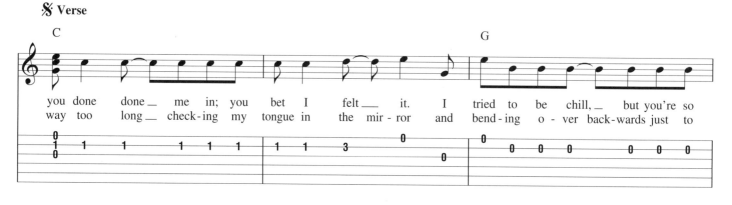

you done done — me in; you bet I felt — it. I tried to be chill, — but you're so
way too long — check-ing my tongue in the mir - ror and bend-ing o - ver back-wards just to

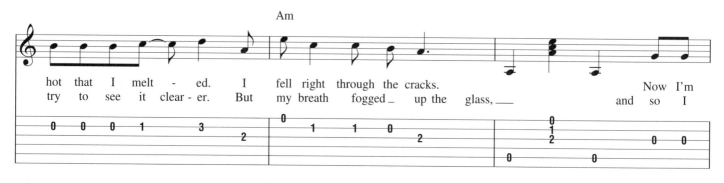

hot that I melt - ed. I fell right through the cracks.   Now I'm
try to see it clear - er. But my breath fogged — up the glass, —   and so I

Copyright © 2008 Goo Eyed Music (ASCAP)
International Copyright Secured All Rights Reserved

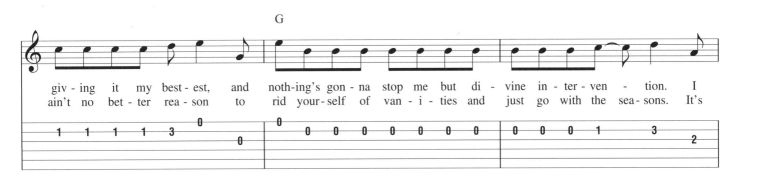

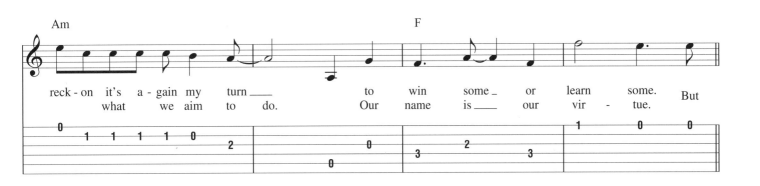

Chorus

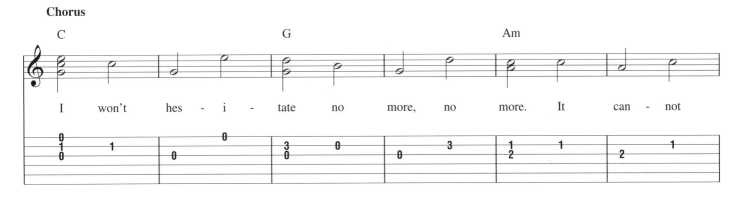

To Coda ⊕

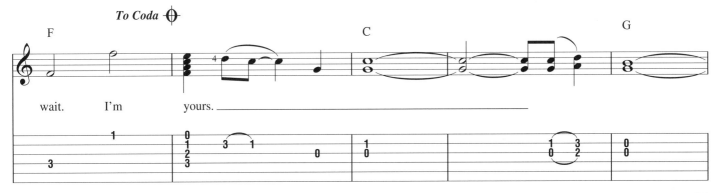

Verse

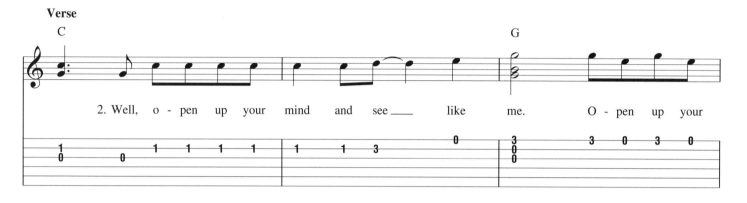

2. Well, o-pen up your mind and see ___ like me. O-pen up your

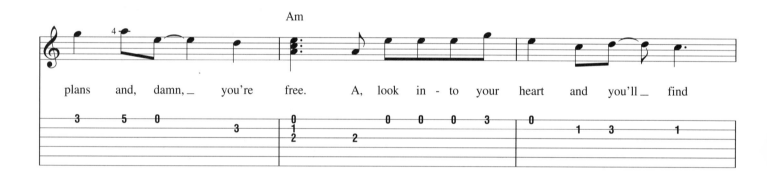

plans and, damn, ___ you're free. A, look in-to your heart and you'll ___ find

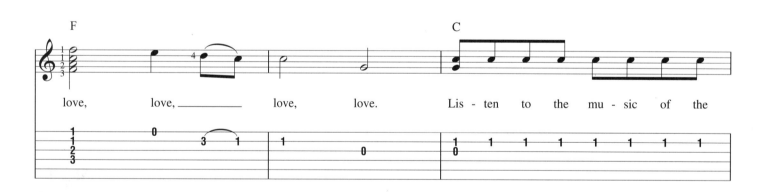

love, love, ___ love, love. Lis-ten to the mu-sic of the

mo-ment; peo-ple dance ___ and sing. We're just one big fam-i-ly, and it's our god-

-for - sak - en right to be loved, loved, _____ loved, loved, loved. _____

Chorus

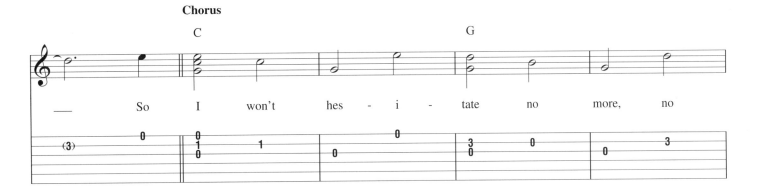

___ So I won't hes - i - tate no more, no

more. It can - not wait. I'm sure _____ there's no need to com - pli -

cate. Our time is short. This is our fate. I'm yours. _____ *Scat...*

Interlude

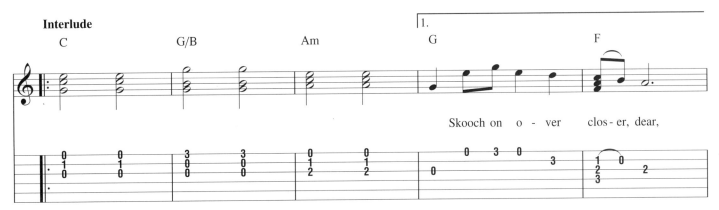

Skooch on o - ver clos - er, dear,

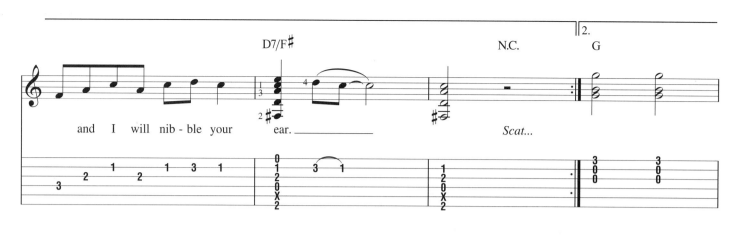

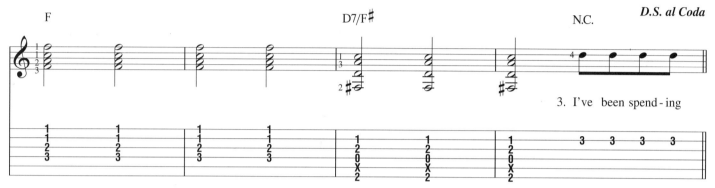

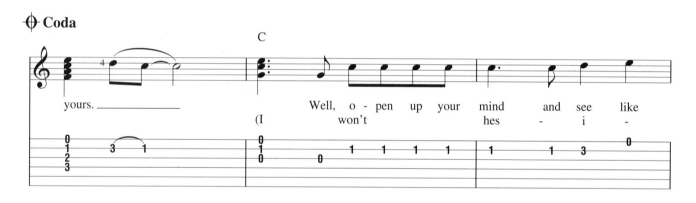

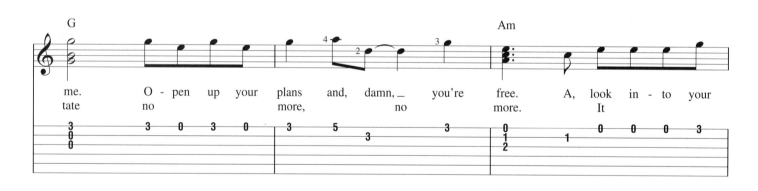

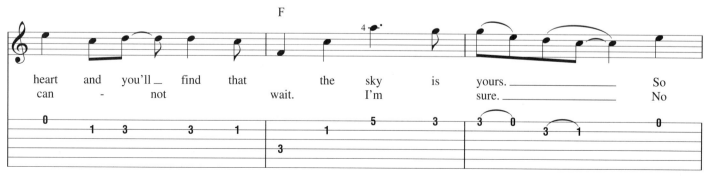

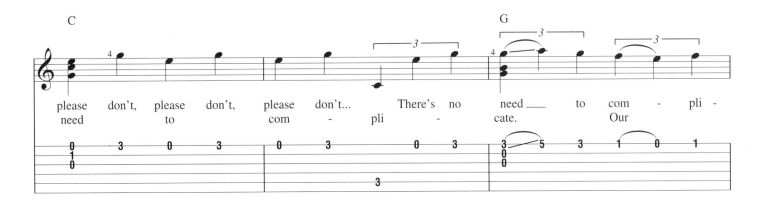

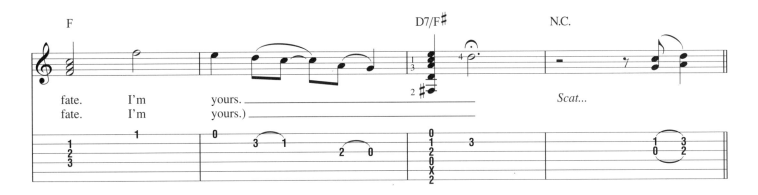

Outro

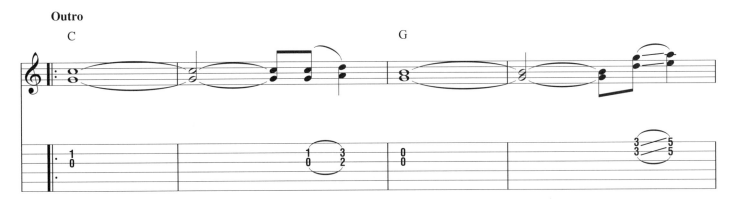

Repeat and fade

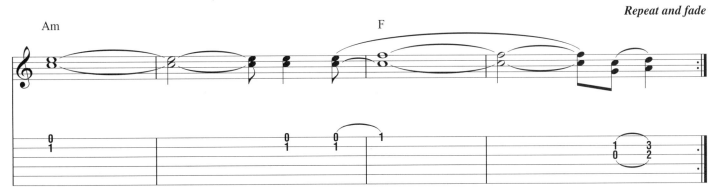

If It Kills Me

Words and Music by Jason Mraz, Martin Terefe and Sacha Skarbek

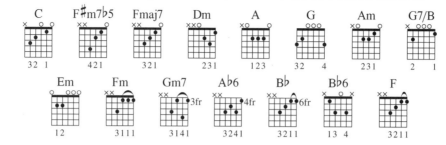

*Capo II

Strum Pattern: 1
Pick Pattern: 5

Verse
Moderately slow

1. Hel - lo. _____ Tell me you know. Yeah, you fig - ured me out.
2. How long _____ can I go _____ on like this, wish-ing to kiss you

*Optional: To match recording, place capo at 2nd fret.

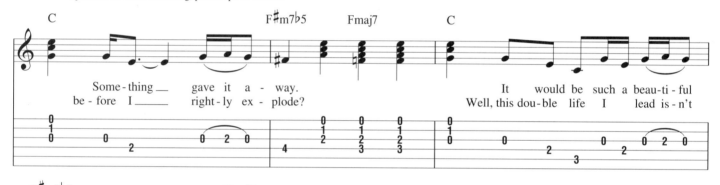

Some - thing _____ gave it a - way. It would be such a beau-ti - ful
be - fore I _____ right-ly ex - plode? Well, this dou-ble life I lead is - n't

mo - ment to see the look on your face. To know that _____ I know that you
health - y for me; in fact, it makes me nerv - ous. If I get caught I could be risk - ing it

know now. _____ And ba - by, that's a case of my wish - ful _____ think - ing.
all. _____ 'Cause may-be there's a lot that I'll miss in _____ case I'm

Copyright © 2008 Goo Eyed Music (ASCAP), Sony/ATV Music Publishing UK Ltd., Key Red Ltd. and Universal Music Publishing Ltd.
All Rights for Sony/ATV Music Publishing UK Ltd. and Key Red Ltd. Administered by Sony/ATV Music Publishing LLC, 8 Music Square West, Nashville, TN 37203
All Rights for Universal Music Publishing Ltd. in the U.S. and Canada Controlled and Administered by Universal - Songs Of PolyGram International, Inc.
International Copyright Secured   All Rights Reserved

You know nothing. / wrong. Well, you and I, why we go carrying on for hours on end.

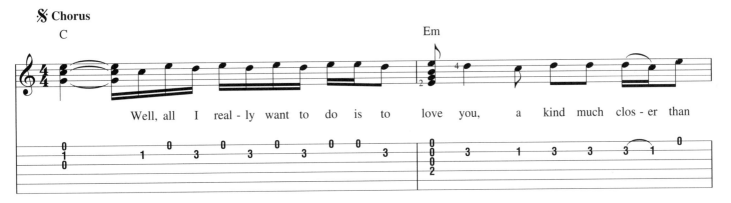

We get along much better than you and your boyfriend.

𝄋 Chorus

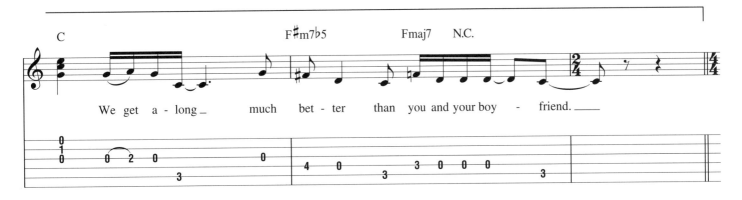

Well, all I really want to do is to love you, a kind much closer than

friends use, but I still can't say it after all we've been through.

And all I really want from you is to feel me as the feeling inside keeps

build - ing. _____ And I will find a way to you if it kills me, ___ if it kills me.

kills me, ___ if it kills me, ___ if it kills me. _____

Bridge

If I should be so bold, I'd ask you to hold _ my heart in your hand; I'd

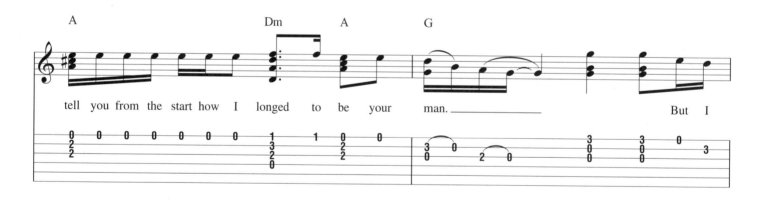

tell you from the start how I longed to be your man. _____ But I

nev - er said a word. I guess I've gone and missed my chance a - gain. _____

Lucky

Words and Music by Jason Mraz, Colbie Caillat and Timothy Fagan

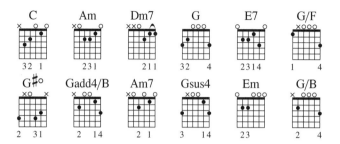

Strum Pattern: 3, 5
Pick Pattern: 3, 6

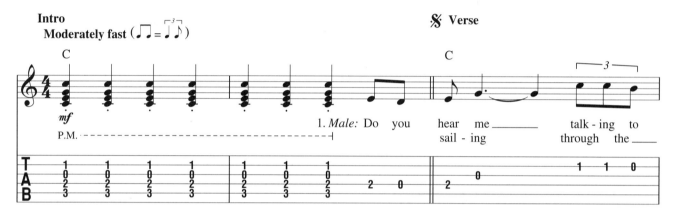

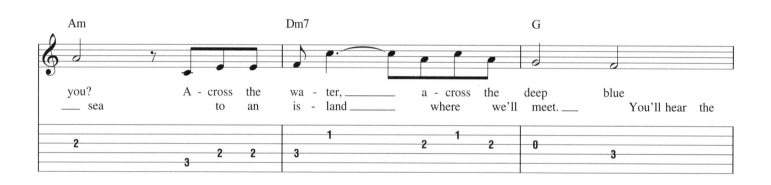

Copyright © 2008 Sony/ATV Music Publishing LLC, Cocomarie Music, Wrunch Time Music and Goo Eyed Music
All Rights on behalf of Sony/ATV Music Publishing LLC, Cocomarie Music and Wrunch Time Music Administered by
Sony/ATV Music Publishing LLC, 8 Music Square West, Nashville, TN 37203
International Copyright Secured   All Rights Reserved

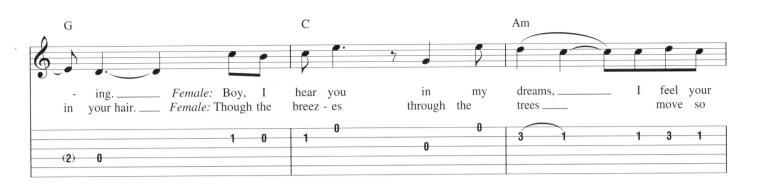

To Coda 1 ⊕

Chorus

*1st time, let chord ring.

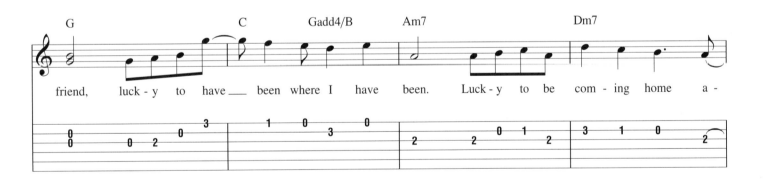

Interlude

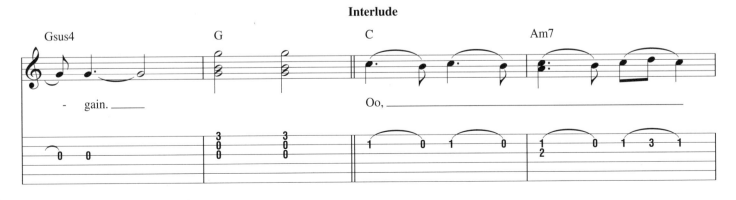

Bridge

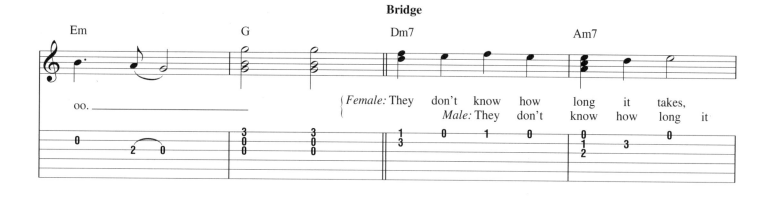

oo. _____

Female: They don't know how long it takes,
Male: They don't know how long it

takes, wait-ing for a love like this. Ev - 'ry time we say good - bye,
wait-ing for a love like this. Ev - 'ry time we say good -

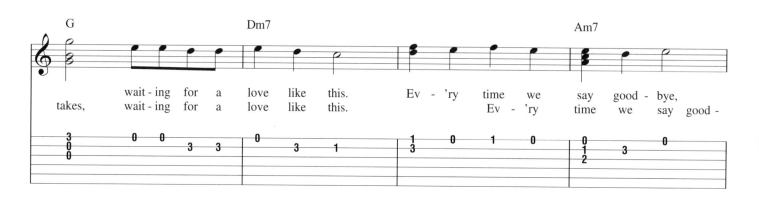

bye, _Both:_ I wish we had one more kiss. I'll wait for you, I prom - ise you I

%. %. Chorus

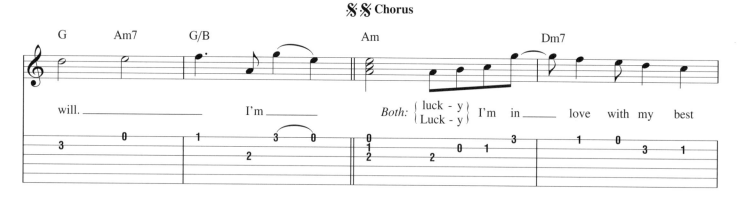

will. _____ I'm _____ _Both:_ { luck - y / Luck - y } I'm in _____ love with my best

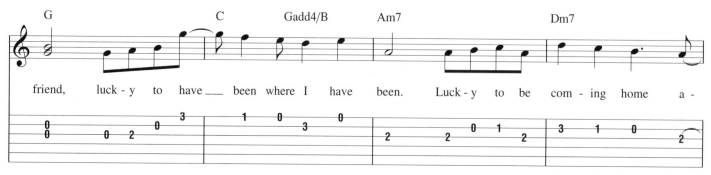

friend, luck - y to have ___ been where I have been. Luck - y to be com - ing home a -

36

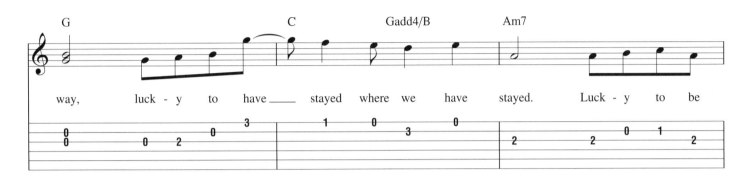

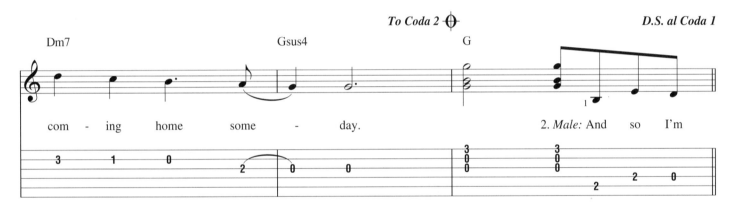

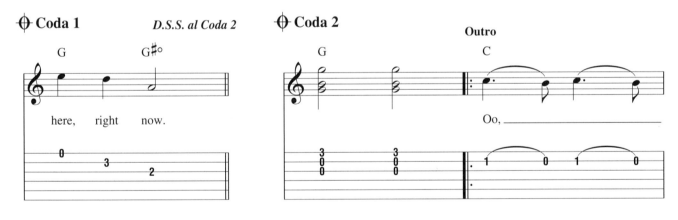

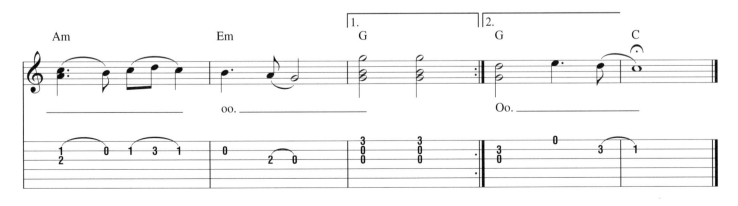

Make It Mine

Words and Music by Jason Mraz

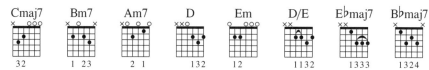

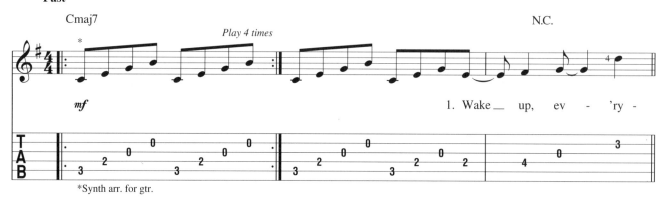

Strum Pattern: 1
Pick Pattern: 1

Intro
Fast

Verse

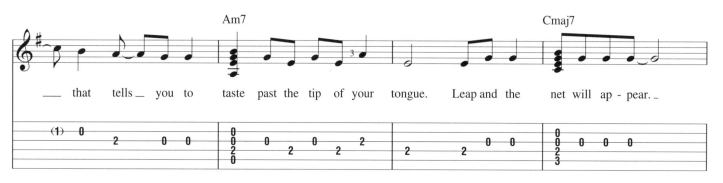

Copyright © 2008 Goo Eyed Music (ASCAP)
International Copyright Secured   All Rights Reserved

Verse

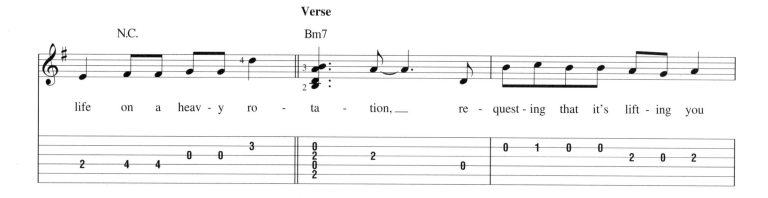

life on a heav-y ro-ta-tion,___ re-quest-ing that it's lift-ing you

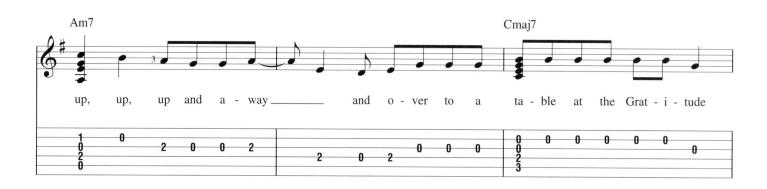

up, up, up and a-way_____ and o-ver to a ta-ble at the Grat-i-tude

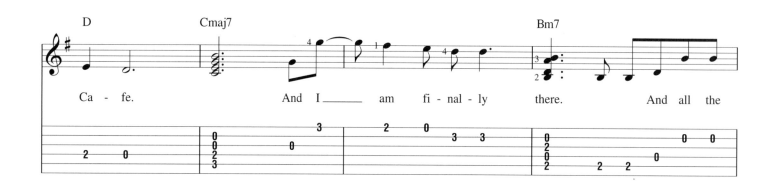

Ca-fe. And I___ am fi-nal-ly there. And all the

an-gels, they'll be sing-ing, ah, I, la, la, la, I, la, la, la,

D.S. al Coda 1

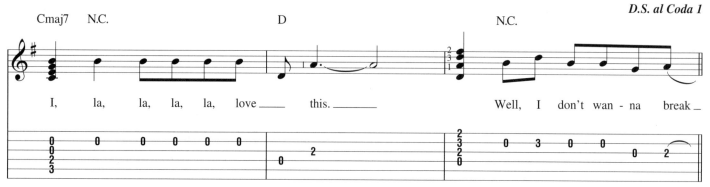

I, la, la, la, la, love___ this._____ Well, I don't wan-na break___

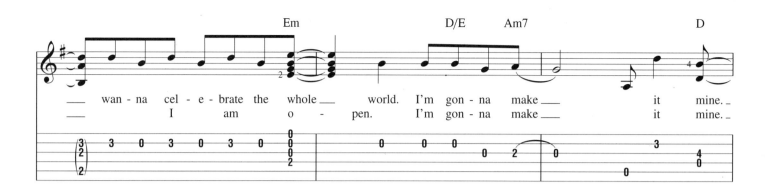

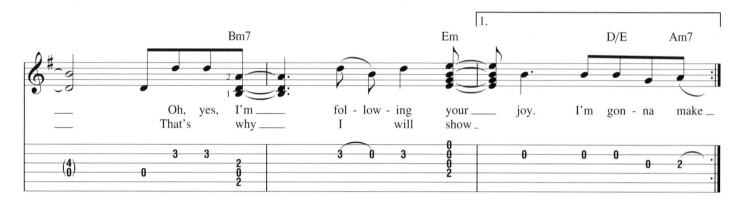

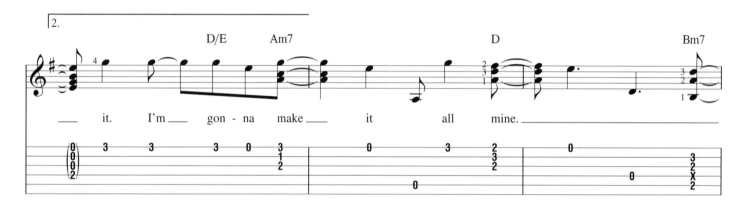

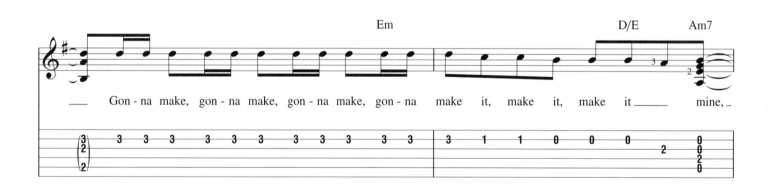

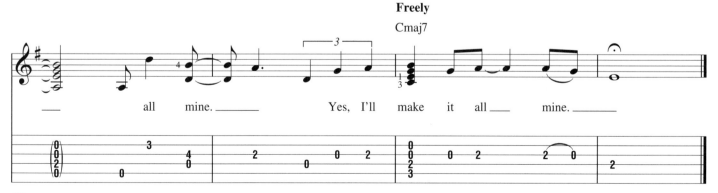

The Woman I Love

Words and Music by Jason Mraz and David Hodges

*Capo IV

Strum Pattern: 6
Pick Pattern: 5

Intro

Moderately slow

*Optional: To match recording, place capo at 4th fret.

Verse

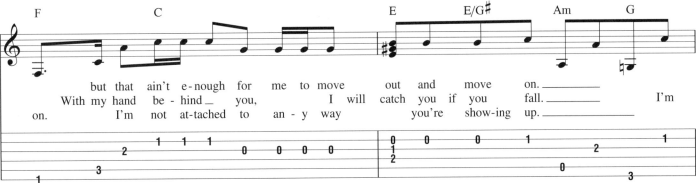

1. May - be I an - noy you with my choic - es.
2. We don't have to hur - ry; you can take as long as you want.
3. I don't wish to change you; you've got it un - der con - trol.

Well, you an - noy me some - times too with your voice, _
I'm hold - ing stead - y _ and my heart's at home. _
You wake up each day dif - f'rent; an - oth - er rea - son for me to keep hold - ing

but that ain't e - nough for me to move out and move on. _
With my hand be - hind _ you, I will catch you if you fall. _ I'm
on. I'm not at - tached to an - y way you're show - ing up. _

Copyright © 2012 Goo Eyed Music (ASCAP), EMI Blackwood Music Inc. (BMI) and 12:06 Publishing (BMI)
All Rights for 12:06 Publishing Controlled and Administered by EMI Blackwood Music Inc.
International Copyright Secured   All Rights Reserved

93 Million Miles

Words and Music by Jason Mraz, Michael Natter and Mike Daly

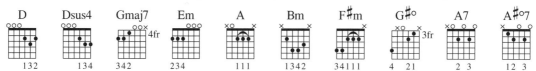

*Drop D tuning, capo I:
(low to high) D-A-D-G-B-E

Strum Pattern: 5
Pick Pattern: 1

Intro

Moderately fast

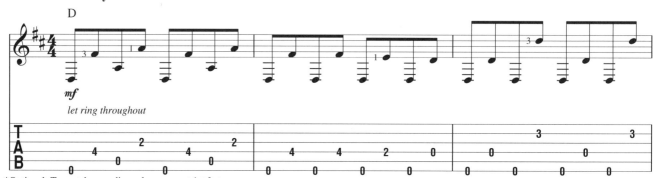

*Optional: To match recording, place capo at 1st fret.

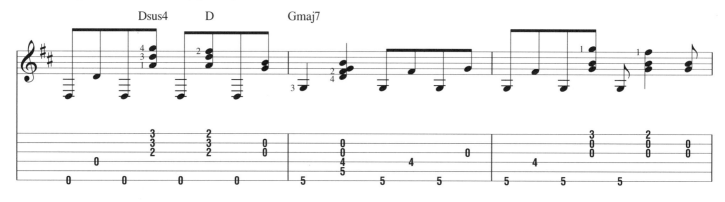

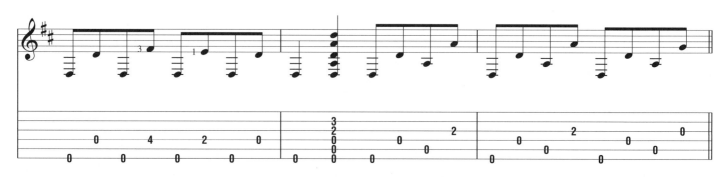

Copyright © 2012 Goo Eyed Music (ASCAP), Great Hooks Music c/o No BS Publishing (ASCAP) and PSYWAR Music Ltd. (ASCAP)
International Copyright Secured   All Rights Reserved

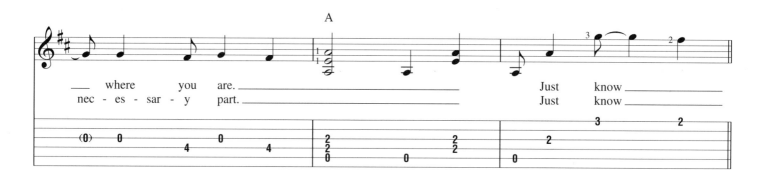

_____ where you are. _____
nec - es - sar - y part. _____ Just know _____

% Chorus

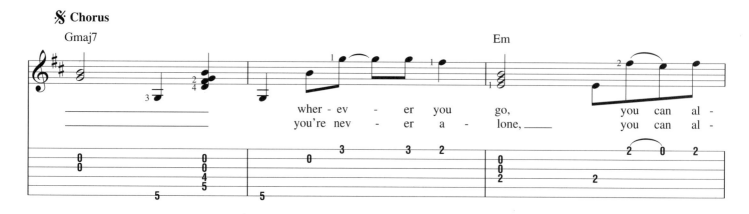

_____
_____ wher - ev - er you go, _____ you can al -
you're nev - er a - lone, _____ you can al -

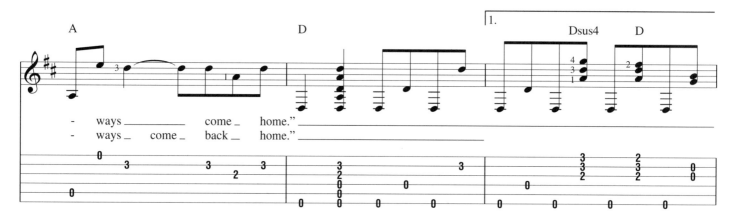

- ways _____ come _ home."
- ways _ come _ back _ home."

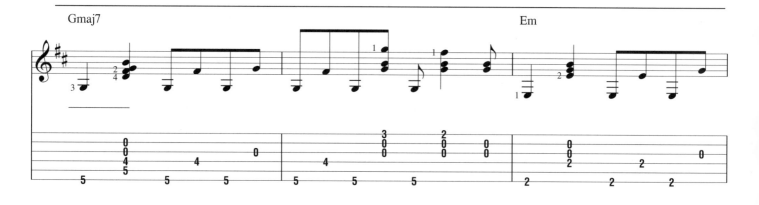

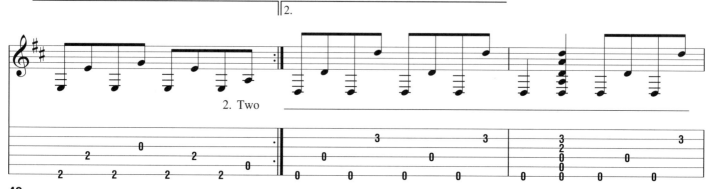

2. Two

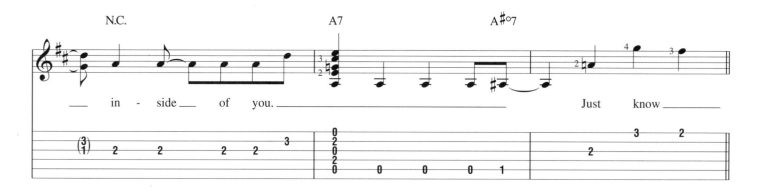

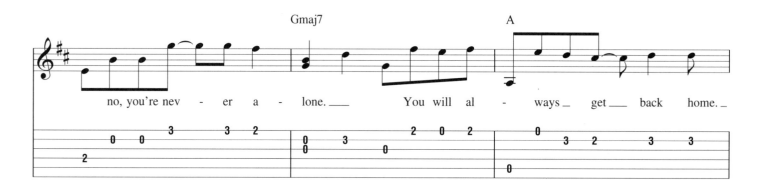

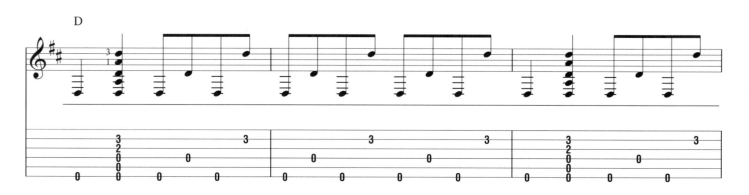

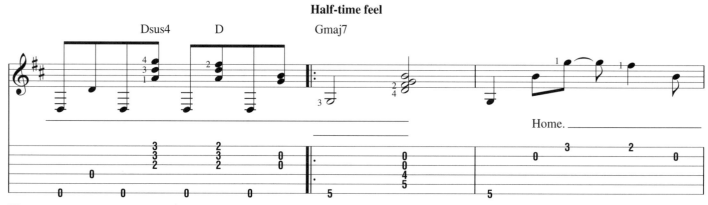

The Remedy (I Won't Worry)

Words and Music by Graham Edwards, Scott Spock, Lauren Christy and Jason Mraz

*Capo III

Strum Pattern: 5
Pick Pattern: 1

Intro
Moderately, in 2

*Optional: To match recording, place capo at 3rd fret.

1. Well, I saw fire-works from the free - way, and be-
2. Well, I heard two men talk-ing on the ra - di - o in a

Copyright © 2002 by Universal Music - MGB Songs, Graham Edwards Songs, Universal Music - Careers,
Scott Spock Songs, Warner-Tamerlane Publishing Corp., Rainbow Fish Publishing and Goo Eyed Music
All Rights for Graham Edwards Songs Administered by Universal Music - MGB Songs
All Rights for Scott Spock Songs Administered by Universal Music - Careers
All Rights for Rainbow Fish Publishing Administered by Warner-Tamerlane Publishing Corp.
International Copyright Secured   All Rights Reserved

hind closed eyes I can-not make them go a - way 'cause you were born on the Fourth of Ju - ly, __
cross - fire kind of new re - al - i - ty show un - cov-er - ing the ways to plan the

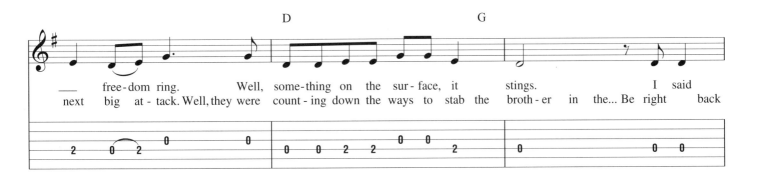

__ free-dom ring. Well, some-thing on the sur - face, it stings. I said
next big at - tack. Well, they were count-ing down the ways to stab the broth - er in the... Be right back

some-thing on the sur-face, well, it kind of makes me nerv-ous. Who says that you de-serve this, and what
__ af - ter this, the un - a - void - a - ble kiss, where the mint - y fresh death breath is

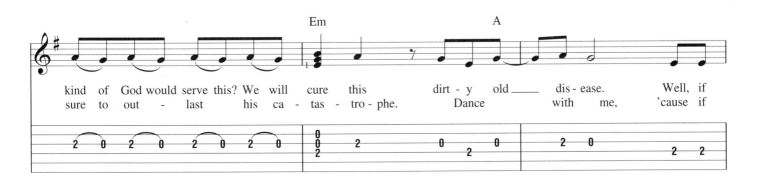

kind of God would serve this? We will cure this dirt - y old ____ dis - ease. Well, if
sure to out - last his ca - tas - tro - phe. Dance with me, 'cause if

Pre-Chorus

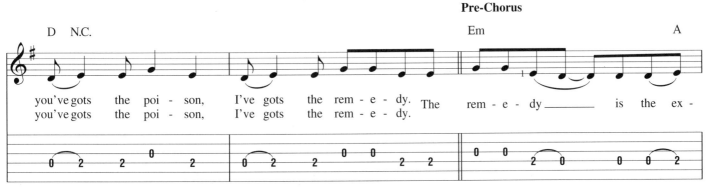

you've gots the poi - son, I've gots the rem - e - dy. The rem - e - dy _____ is the ex -
you've gots the poi - son, I've gots the rem - e - dy.

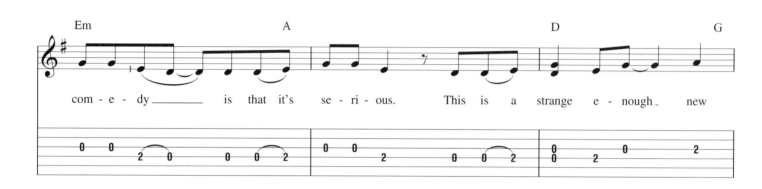

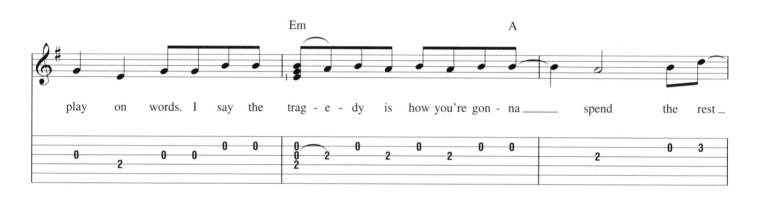

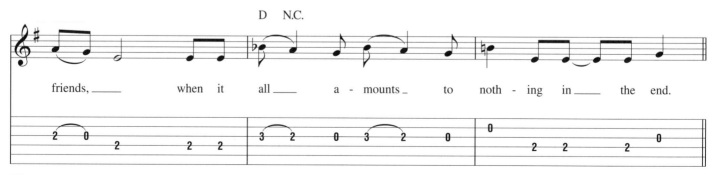

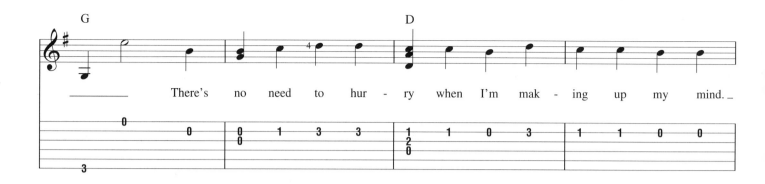

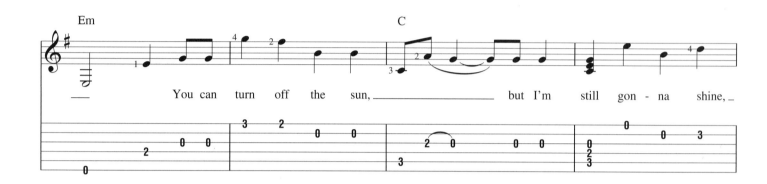

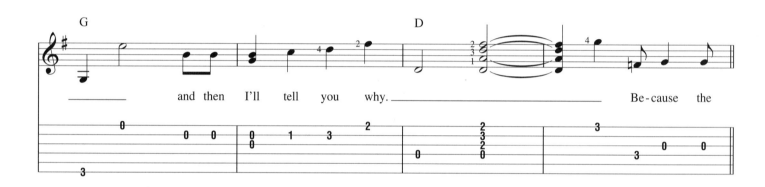

Pre-Chorus

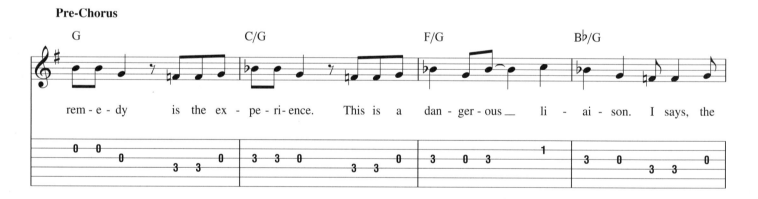

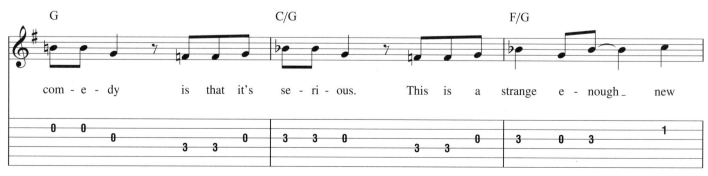

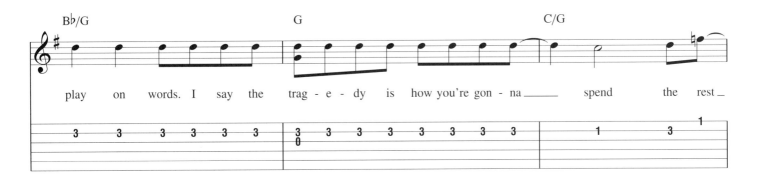

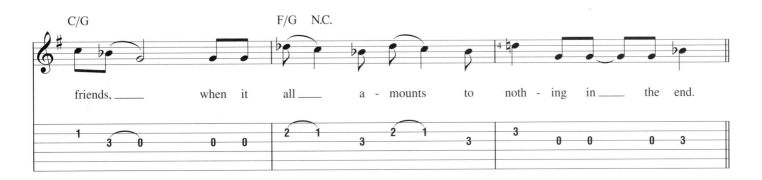

Outro-Chorus

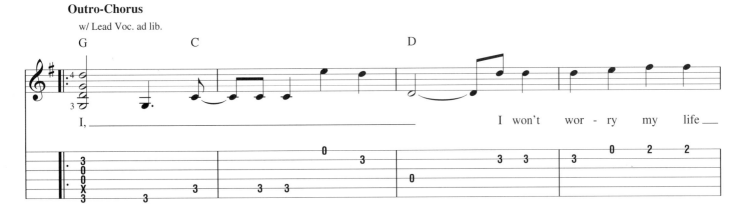

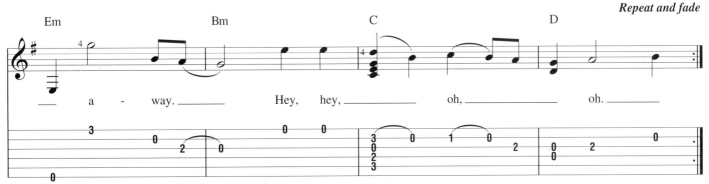

You and I Both

Words and Music by Jason Mraz

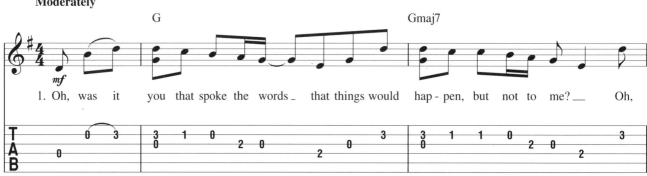

Strum Pattern: 2
Pick Pattern: 2

Verse
Moderately

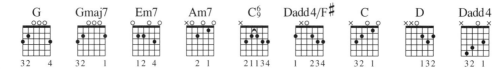

1. Oh, was it you that spoke the words that things would hap-pen, but not to me? Oh,

things are gon-na hap-pen nat-'ral-ly. Oh, tak-ing your ad-vice, and I'm

look-ing on the bright side and bal-anc-ing the, the whole thing. Oh, but at

of-ten times those words, they get tan-gled up in a lines; and the bright light turns to night, oh, un-

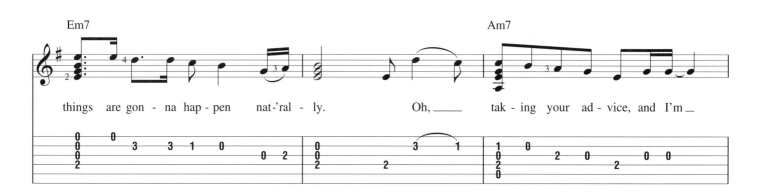
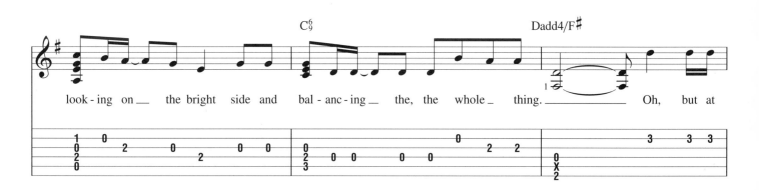
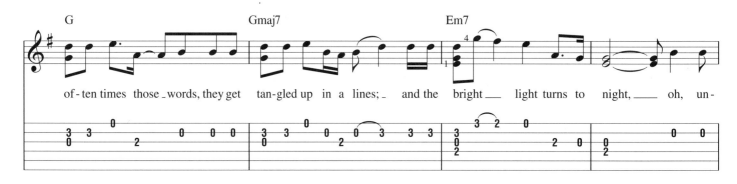

Copyright © 2002 Goo Eyed Music (ASCAP)
International Copyright Secured   All Rights Reserved

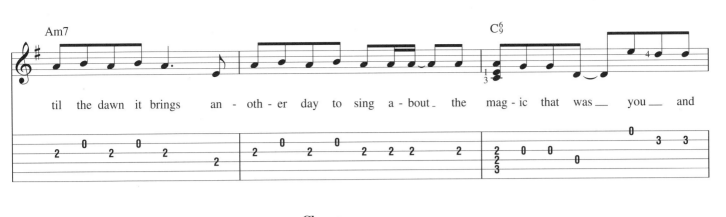

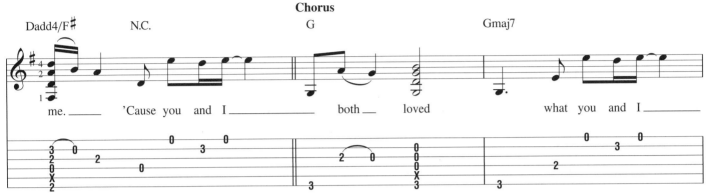

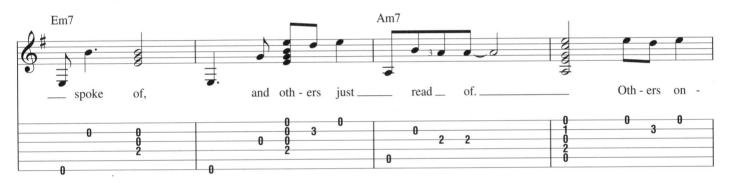

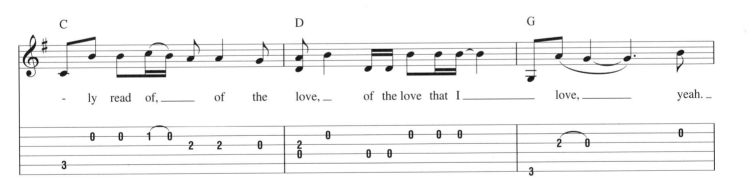

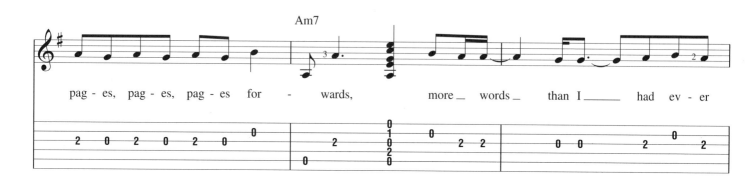

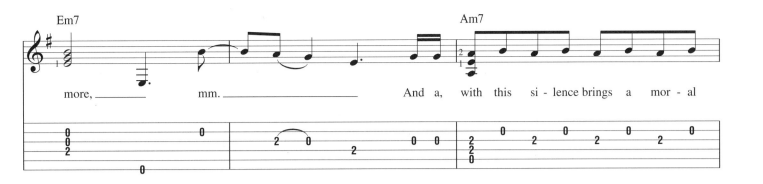

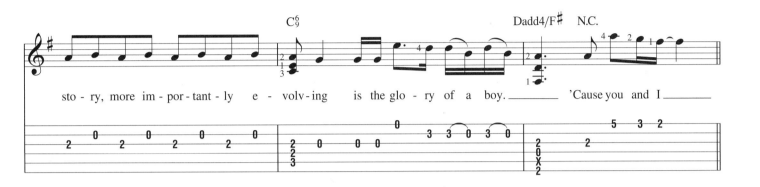

§ Chorus

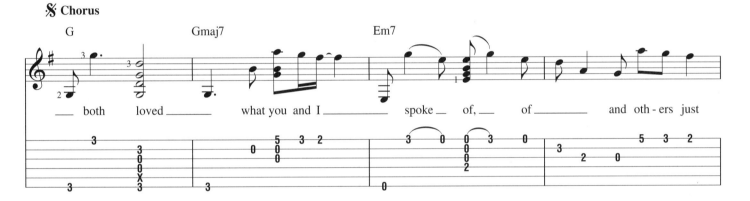

To Coda ⊕

*Let chord ring.

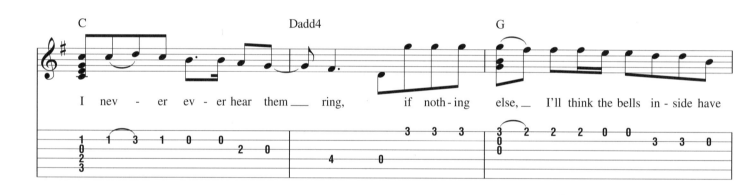

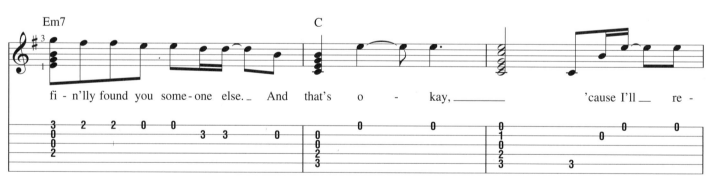

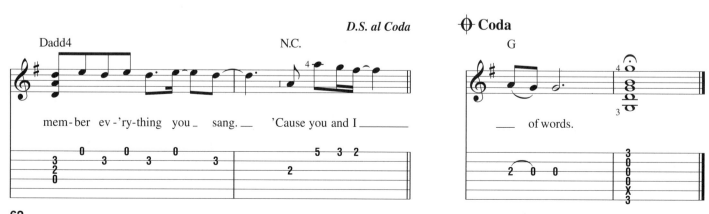

EASY GUITAR WITH NOTES & TAB

This series features simplified arrangements with notes, tab, chord charts, and strum and pick patterns.

MIXED FOLIOS

00702287 Acoustic	$14.99
00702002 Acoustic Rock Hits for Easy Guitar	$12.95
00702166 All-Time Best Guitar Collection	$19.99
00699665 Beatles Best	$12.95
00702232 Best Acoustic Songs for Easy Guitar	$12.99
00702233 Best Hard Rock Songs	$14.99
00703055 The Big Book of Nursery Rhymes & Children's Songs	$14.99
00322179 The Big Easy Book of Classic Rock Guitar	$24.95
00698978 Big Christmas Collection	$16.95
00702394 Bluegrass Songs for Easy Guitar	$12.99
00703387 Celtic Classics	$14.99
00118314 Chart Hits of 2012-2013	$14.99
00702149 Children's Christian Songbook	$7.95
00702237 Christian Acoustic Favorites	$12.95
00702028 Christmas Classics	$7.95
00101779 Christmas Guitar	$14.99
00702185 Christmas Hits	$9.95
00702016 Classic Blues for Easy Guitar	$12.95
00702141 Classic Rock	$8.95
00702203 CMT's 100 Greatest Country Songs	$27.95
00702283 The Contemporary Christian Collection	$16.99
00702006 Contemporary Christian Favorites	$9.95
00702239 Country Classics for Easy Guitar	$19.99
00702282 Country Hits of 2009–2010	$14.99

00702240 Country Hits of 2007–2008	$12.95
00702225 Country Hits of '06–'07	$12.95
00702085 Disney Movie Hits	$12.95
00702257 Easy Acoustic Guitar Songs	$14.99
00702280 Easy Guitar Tab White Pages	$29.99
00702212 Essential Christmas	$9.95
00702041 Favorite Hymns for Easy Guitar	$9.95
00702281 4 Chord Rock	$9.99
00702286 Glee	$16.99
00699374 Gospel Favorites	$14.95
00702160 The Great American Country Songbook	$15.99
00702050 Great Classical Themes for Easy Guitar	$6.95
00702116 Greatest Hymns for Guitar	$8.95
00702130 The Groovy Years	$9.95
00702184 Guitar Instrumentals	$9.95
00702046 Hits of the '70s for Easy Guitar	$8.95
00702273 Irish Songs	$12.99
00702275 Jazz Favorites for Easy Guitar	$14.99
00702274 Jazz Standards for Easy Guitar	$14.99
00702162 Jumbo Easy Guitar Songbook	$19.95
00702258 Legends of Rock	$14.99
00702261 Modern Worship Hits	$14.99
00702189 MTV's 100 Greatest Pop Songs	$24.95
00702272 1950s Rock	$14.99
00702271 1960s Rock	$14.99
00702270 1970s Rock	$14.99

00702269 1980s Rock	$14.99
00702268 1990s Rock	$14.99
00109725 Once	$14.99
00702187 Selections from O Brother Where Art Thou?	$12.95
00702178 100 Songs for Kids	$12.95
00702515 Pirates of the Caribbean	$12.99
00702125 Praise and Worship for Guitar	$9.95
00702155 Rock Hits for Guitar	$9.95
00702285 Southern Rock Hits	$12.99
00702866 Theme Music	$12.99
00121535 30 Easy Celtic Guitar Solos	$14.99
00702124 Today's Christian Rock – 2nd Edition	$9.95
00702220 Today's Country Hits	$9.95
00702198 Today's Hits for Guitar	$9.95
00702217 Top Christian Hits	$12.95
00702235 Top Christian Hits of '07–'08	$14.95
00103626 Top Hits of 2012	$14.99
00702294 Top Worship Hits	$14.99
00702206 Very Best of Rock	$9.95
00702255 VH1's 100 Greatest Hard Rock Songs	$27.99
00702175 VH1's 100 Greatest Songs of Rock and Roll	$24.95
00702253 Wicked	$12.99

ARTIST COLLECTIONS

00702267 AC/DC for Easy Guitar	$15.99
00702598 Adele for Easy Guitar	$14.99
00702001 Best of Aerosmith	$16.95
00702040 Best of the Allman Brothers	$14.99
00702865 J.S. Bach for Easy Guitar	$12.99
00702169 Best of The Beach Boys	$12.99
00702292 The Beatles — 1	$19.99
00702201 The Essential Black Sabbath	$12.95
00702140 Best of Brooks & Dunn	$10.95
02501615 Zac Brown Band — The Foundation	$16.99
02501621 Zac Brown Band — You Get What You Give	$16.99
00702095 Best of Mariah Carey	$12.95
00702043 Best of Johnny Cash	$16.99
00702033 Best of Steven Curtis Chapman	$14.95
00702291 Very Best of Coldplay	$12.99
00702263 Best of Casting Crowns	$12.99
00702090 Eric Clapton's Best	$10.95
00702086 Eric Clapton — from the Album Unplugged	$10.95
00702202 The Essential Eric Clapton	$12.95
00702250 blink-182 — Greatest Hits	$12.99
00702053 Best of Patsy Cline	$10.95
00702229 The Very Best of Creedence Clearwater Revival	$14.99
00702145 Best of Jim Croce	$12.99
00702278 Crosby, Stills & Nash	$12.99
00702219 David Crowder*Band Collection	$12.95
00702122 The Doors for Easy Guitar	$12.99
00702276 Fleetwood Mac — Easy Guitar Collection	$12.99
00702190 Best of Pat Green	$19.95

00702136 Best of Merle Haggard	$12.99
00702243 Hannah Montana	$14.95
00702227 Jimi Hendrix — Smash Hits	$14.99
00702288 Best of Hillsong United	$12.99
00702236 Best of Antonio Carlos Jobim	$12.95
00702245 Elton John — Greatest Hits 1970–2002	$14.99
00702204 Robert Johnson	$9.95
00702277 Best of Jonas Brothers	$14.99
00702234 Selections from Toby Keith — 35 Biggest Hits	$12.95
00702003 Kiss	$9.95
00702193 Best of Jennifer Knapp	$12.95
00702216 Lynyrd Skynyrd	$15.99
00702182 The Essential Bob Marley	$12.95
00702346 Bruno Mars — Doo-Wops & Hooligans	$12.99
00702248 Paul McCartney — All the Best	$14.99
00702129 Songs of Sarah McLachlan	$12.95
02501316 Metallica — Death Magnetic	$15.95
00702209 Steve Miller Band — Young Hearts (Greatest Hits)	$12.95
00702096 Best of Nirvana	$14.95
00702211 The Offspring — Greatest Hits	$12.95
00702030 Best of Roy Orbison	$12.95
00702144 Best of Ozzy Osbourne	$14.99
00702279 Tom Petty	$12.99
00102911 Pink Floyd	$16.99
00702139 Elvis Country Favorites	$9.95
00702293 The Very Best of Prince	$12.99
00699415 Best of Queen for Guitar	$14.99
00109279 Best of R.E.M.	$14.99

00702208 Red Hot Chili Peppers — Greatest Hits	$12.95
00702093 Rolling Stones Collection	$17.95
00702092 Best of the Rolling Stones	$14.99
00702196 Best of Bob Seger	$12.95
00702252 Frank Sinatra — Nothing But the Best	$12.99
00702010 Best of Rod Stewart	$14.95
00702049 Best of George Strait	$12.95
00702259 Taylor Swift for Easy Guitar	$14.99
00702260 Taylor Swift – Fearless	$12.99
00115960 Taylor Swift — Red	$16.99
00702290 Taylor Swift — Speak Now	$14.99
00702223 Chris Tomlin — Arriving	$12.95
00702262 Chris Tomlin Collection	$14.99
00702226 Chris Tomlin — See the Morning	$12.95
00702427 U2 — 18 Singles	$14.99
00702108 Best of Stevie Ray Vaughan	$10.95
00702123 Best of Hank Williams	$12.99
00702111 Stevie Wonder — Guitar Collection	$9.95
00702228 Neil Young — Greatest Hits	$15.99
00119133 Neil Young – Harvest	$14.99
00702188 Essential ZZ Top	$10.95

Prices, contents and availability subject to change without notice.

HAL•LEONARD® CORPORATION

7777 W. BLUEMOUND RD. P.O. BOX 13819 MILWAUKEE, WI 53213

Visit Hal Leonard online at **www.halleonard.com**

0713

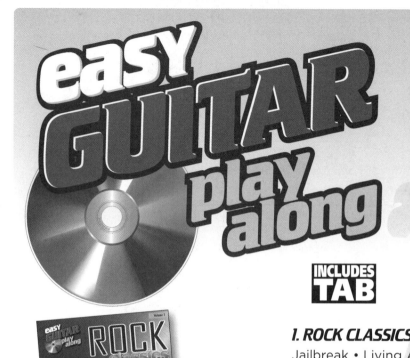

easy GUITAR play along

INCLUDES TAB

The *easy GUITAR play along* ® Series features streamlined transcriptions of your favorite songs. Just follow the tab, listen to the CD to hear how the guitar should sound, and then play along using the backing tracks. The CD is playable on any CD player, and is also enhanced to include the Amazing Slowdowner technology so Mac and PC users can adjust the recording to any tempo without changing the pitch!

1. ROCK CLASSICS
Jailbreak • Living After Midnight • Mississippi Queen • Rocks Off • Runnin' Down a Dream • Smoke on the Water • Strutter • Up Around the Bend.

00702560 Book/CD Pack.......$14.99

2. ACOUSTIC TOP HITS
About a Girl • I'm Yours • The Lazy Song • The Scientist • 21 Guns • Upside Down • What I Got • Wonderwall.

00702569 Book/CD Pack.......$14.99

3. ROCK HITS
All the Small Things • Best of You • Brain Stew (The Godzilla Remix) • Californication • Island in the Sun • Plush • Smells like Teen Spirit • Use Somebody.

00702570 Book/CD Pack.......$14.99

4. ROCK 'N' ROLL
Blue Suede Shoes • I Get Around • I'm a Believer • Jailhouse Rock • Oh, Pretty Woman • Peggy Sue • Runaway • Wake up Little Susie.

00702572 Book/CD Pack........$14.99

5. ULTIMATE ACOUSTIC
Against the Wind • Babe, I'm Gonna Leave You • Come Monday • Free Fallin' • Give a Little Bit • Have You Ever Seen the Rain? • New Kid in Town • We Can Work It Out.

00702573 Book/CD Pack........$14.99

6. CHRISTMAS SONGS
Have Yourself a Merry Little Christmas • A Holly Jolly Christmas • The Little Drummer Boy • Run Rudolph Run • Santa Claus Is Comin' to Town • Silver and Gold • Sleigh Ride • Winter Wonderland.

00101879 Book/CD Pack.........$14.99

7. BLUES SONGS FOR BEGINNERS
Come On (Part 1) • Double Trouble • Gangster of Love • I'm Ready • Let Me Love You Baby • Mary Had a Little Lamb • San-Ho-Zay • T-Bone Shuffle.

00103235 Book/CD Pack.....$14.99

8. ACOUSTIC SONGS FOR BEGINNERS
Barely Breathing • Drive • Everlong • Good Riddance (Time of Your Life) • Hallelujah • Hey There Delilah • Lake of Fire • Photograph.

00103240 Book/CD Pack.....$14.99

9. ROCK SONGS FOR BEGINNERS
Are You Gonna Be My Girl • Buddy Holly • Everybody Hurts • In Bloom • Otherside • The Rock Show • Santa Monica • When I Come Around.

00103255 Book/CD Pack.....$14.99

Prices, contents, and availability subject to change without notice.

HAL•LEONARD® CORPORATION
7777 W. BLUEMOUND RD. P.O. BOX 13819
MILWAUKEE, WISCONSIN 53213

www.halleonard.com

0113